Grandmother's Journal

YOUR CHERISHED MEMORIES
IN YOUR OWN WORDS

COUNTRYMAN
®

Nashville, Tennessee

www.jcountryman.com

Project Editor: Michelle Orr

Designed by LJDesigns, ljdsgn@swbell.net

ISBN 14041-0197-7

Printed and bound in the United States

Cherish all your happy moments: they make a fine cushion for old age.

BOOTH TARKINGTON

INTRODUCTION

In January we think of new beginnings; in February of valentines, first dates, and first kisses. Does ever a June pass without thoughts of our own wedding day? Surely summer evokes backseat memories of seemingly unending trips to Grandma's house or the beach. And don't November and December bring to mind family traditions and celebrations held tightly through the years?

Like ivy on the garden trellis, our lives are inescapably entwined with the seasons and months of the year. That is why we have designed this grandmother's memory journal in a twelve-month format. Each month features intriguing questions with space to write a personal answer. Questions explore family history, childhood memories, lighthearted incidents, cherished traditions, and the dreams and spiritual adventures encountered in a lifetime of living.

Whether you choose to complete the journal in a few days, weeks, or over the course of a year, the questions will take you on a journey through the times and seasons of your life. This makes a tangible family record to pass on as a gift to your children and grandchildren, a loving memoir of written words that are windows to a grandmother's heart.

No matter what your age, memory and reminiscence open a richer, fuller understanding of who you are as a family. Let this memory journal be a starting point-a door into discussing and sharing the unique qualities of your life. May *Grandmother's Journal* draw you closer to each other as you share the experiences of a lifetime.

PERSONAL PORTRAIT

your full given name _____

your date of birth _____

your place of birth _____

your mother's full name _____

the place and date of her birth _____

_____

your father's full name _____

the place and date of his birth _____

_____

the names of your paternal grandparents _____

_____

the places and dates of their births _____

_____

the names of your maternal grandparents _____

_____

the places and dates of their birth _____

_____

_____

the names of your siblings _____

_____

_____

the places and dates of their births _____

_____

_____

the place and date of your marriage _____

_____

the full given name of your husband _____

_____

the names and birth dates of your children _____

_____

_____

_____

the names and birth dates of your grandchildren _____

_____

_____

_____

WHAT IS YOUR FAVORITE

flower _____

perfume _____

color _____

hymn or song _____

_____

_____

book _____

author _____

Scripture, saying or quotation _____

_____

_____

holiday _____

dessert _____

vacation spot _____

_____

type of food _____

sport _____

leisure activity _____

FAVORITE
PHOTO

JANUARY

What is a Grandmother?

She is warmth and cheer

and laughter —Someone

who does loving things you

think about long after.

AUTHOR UNKNOWN

What was your favorite pastime as a child? _____

_____

_____

_____

_____

_____

_____

_____

_____

_____

_____

_____

_____

_____

_____

_____

_____

What games did you play? _____

_____

_____

_____

_____

_____

_____

_____

What was your favorite doll or toy? _____

_____

_____

_____

_____

_____

_____

_____

_____

January

Who gave you your name and why? _____

_____

_____

_____

_____

_____

_____

Did you have a nickname? _____

How did you get it? _____

_____

_____

_____

_____

_____

_____

_____

Describe your childhood home. _____

_____

_____

_____

_____

_____

_____

_____

What was your favorite room? _____

_____

_____

_____

_____

_____

_____

_____

_____

What was the silliest thing you ever did as a child?

_____

_____

_____

_____

_____

_____

_____

_____

_____

_____

_____

_____

_____

_____

What were Sundays like as a child? _____

    Did you go to church? _____

    Visit grandparents? _____

    Was there a big family dinner? _____

_____

_____

_____

_____

_____

_____

_____

_____

_____

_____

_____

_____

_____

January

Where did your father go to work every day and what did he do? _____

_____

_____

_____

_____

_____

_____

_____

_____

Share the most wonderful thing about your father.

_____

_____

_____

_____

_____

_____

How did your mother spend her day? Did she have a job or do volunteer work outside the home?

_____

_____

_____

_____

_____

_____

_____

Share the most wonderful thing about your mother.

_____

_____

_____

_____

_____

_____

What were some of your favorite treats as a child?

How much did they cost? _____

_____

_____

_____

_____

_____

_____

_____

_____

_____

_____

_____

_____

_____

_____

January

Did you have a favorite bedtime story or a prayer that
you said before you went to sleep? _____

Who tucked you in? _____

_____

_____

_____

_____

_____

_____

_____

_____

_____

_____

_____

_____

_____

Describe the day your first child was born.

_____

_____

_____

_____

_____

_____

_____

_____

Describe the day your first grandchild was born.

_____

_____

_____

_____

_____

_____

_____

_____

Describe your grandparents' houses. _____

    Did you visit them often? _____

    Why or why not? _____

_____

_____

_____

_____

_____

_____

_____

_____

_____

_____

_____

_____

_____

January

List one special memory about
each of your brothers and sisters.

_____

_____

_____

_____

_____

_____

_____

_____

_____

_____

_____

_____

_____

_____

_____

_____

_____

_____

Recall for me some of the most important lessons you have learned in life. _____

_____

_____

_____

_____

_____

_____

_____

_____

_____

_____

_____

_____

_____

_____

_____

FEBRUARY

Grandmas hold our tiny

hands for just a little while

. . . but our hearts forever.

AUTHOR UNKNOWN

Who have you turned to for _____

advice or guidance in your life? _____

_____

_____

_____

_____

_____

What advice that was given would _____

you pass along to your grandchildren? _____

_____

_____

_____

_____

_____

_____

_____

As a young girl, did you participate in church, scouting, or some other organization or activity? _____

_____

_____

_____

_____

_____

How important a role did that play in your life? _____

_____

_____

_____

_____

_____

_____

_____

_____

February

Do you remember a special Bible _____

or storybook from your childhood? _____

    Who gave it to you? _____

    Do you still have it? _____

_____

_____

_____

_____

_____

_____

_____

_____

_____

_____

_____

_____

_____

Describe a memorable Valentine you received. _____

_____

_____

_____

_____

_____

_____

Describe a memorable Valentine you gave to someone.

_____

_____

_____

_____

_____

_____

_____

_____

How far did you have to travel to attend elementary school and high school, and how did you get there? _____

_____

_____

_____

_____

_____

_____

_____

_____

_____

_____

_____

_____

_____

_____

_____

What scent or sound immediately

takes you back to childhood?

Describe the feeling it evokes.

February

What was your favorite meal when you were a child?

What made it your favorite? _____

_____

_____

_____

_____

_____

_____

_____

_____

What is your favorite meal to fix _____

for your children and grandchildren? _____

_____

_____

_____

_____

_____

_____

What was the name of your favorite pet?

Why was it your favorite? _____

_____

_____

_____

_____

_____

_____

_____

_____

Share some names of other pets you had growing up.

_____

_____

_____

_____

_____

What chores did you have to do when you were growing up?

Did you get an allowance? _____

How much was it? _____

_____

_____

_____

_____

_____

_____

_____

_____

_____

_____

_____

_____

_____

_____

Tell me about your first job. _____

_____

_____

_____

_____

_____

_____

_____

_____

_____

_____

_____

_____

_____

_____

_____

_____

_____

February

Share your favorite memory of each of your children.

_____

_____

_____

_____

_____

_____

_____

_____

_____

_____

_____

_____

_____

_____

_____

_____

Did you ever meet someone famous? _____

_____

_____
_____
_____
_____
_____
_____
_____
_____
_____
_____
_____
_____
_____
_____
_____
_____
_____

MARCH

Youth lives on hope,

old age on remembrance.

ANONYMOUS
(FRENCH PROVERB)

March

Can you recall a surprise visit from family or friends?

_____

_____

_____

_____

_____

_____

_____

_____

_____

_____

_____

_____

_____

_____

_____

_____

What cute little quote _____

do you remember from _____

each of your children? _____

_____

_____

_____

_____

_____

_____

_____

_____

_____

_____

_____

_____

What did you want to be when you grew up?

How old were you? _____

Did that change over the years? _____

_____

_____

_____

_____

_____

_____

_____

_____

_____

_____

_____

_____

_____

What kinds of things do you enjoy _____

doing with your grandchildren? _____

_____

_____

_____

_____

_____

_____

Do you have a special place you like to take them? ___

_____

_____

_____

_____

_____

_____

_____

_____

What was your favorite subject in elementary school and in high school? _____

_____

_____

_____

_____

_____

_____

Who was your favorite teacher? _____

Why? _____

_____

_____

_____

_____

_____

_____

Describe one of your favorite dress-up outfits as a child.

On what occasions would you wear it? _____

_____

_____

_____

_____

_____

_____

_____

_____

_____

_____

_____

_____

_____

_____

_____

March

Did you ever have a special hideaway or playhouse?

What made it special? _____

_____

_____

_____

_____

_____

_____

_____

_____

_____

_____

_____

_____

_____

_____

What extracurricular activities were you _____

involved in during high school? _____

    Why did you choose those activities? _____

_____

_____

_____

_____

_____

_____

_____

_____

_____

_____

_____

_____

_____

What special song or
saying did you enjoy
teaching your children
and grandchildren?

What was the hardest lesson to teach your kids? _____

_____

_____

_____

_____

_____

_____

_____

_____

_____

_____

_____

_____

_____

_____

_____

March

When did you have your first date? _____

Tell me about it. _____

_____

_____

_____

_____

_____

_____

_____

_____

_____

_____

_____

_____

_____

_____

_____

What do you remember about your first kiss?

Tell me about your first boyfriend.

What did you do to celebrate birthdays when you were growing up? _____

_____

_____

_____

_____

_____

_____

_____

_____

_____

_____

_____

_____

_____

Record some party planning tips that you have found

helpful: _____

_____

_____

_____

_____

_____

_____

What foods do you like to serve at a party? _____

Share your favorite recipe. _____

_____

_____

_____

_____

_____

_____

APRIL

The simplest toy,

one which even the youngest

child can operate,

is called a grandparent.

SAM LEVENSON

April

What were some of the most memorable books you read as a child? _____

_____

_____

_____

_____

_____

_____

_____

What was your favorite book to read to your children?

_____

_____

_____

_____

_____

_____

_____

Tell about an award or special _____

recognition you have received. _____

_____

_____

_____

_____

_____

_____

_____

_____

_____

_____

_____

_____

_____

_____

What were your family finances _____

like when you were growing up? _____

How did that affect you? _____

_____

_____

_____

_____

_____

_____

_____

_____

_____

_____

_____

_____

_____

_____

Share some financial lessons you _____

have learned throughout life. _____

_____

_____

_____

_____

_____

_____

_____

_____

_____

_____

_____

_____

_____

_____

_____

_____

_____

April

What mischievous childhood
experience do you remember?

What meaningful advice did you receive from an adult?

What were the circumstances? _____

_____

_____

_____

_____

_____

_____

_____

_____

_____

_____

_____

_____

_____

_____

What advice do you want to pass along to your grandchildren about being a good parent? ———

_____

_____

_____

_____

_____

_____

_____

_____

_____

_____

_____

_____

_____

_____

_____

What similarities do you see in your children and your
grandchildren? _____

_____

_____

_____

_____

_____

_____

_____

_____

_____

_____

_____

_____

_____

_____

_____

April

What things do you wish you had done in childhood or adolescence? _____

_____

_____

_____

_____

_____

_____

_____

_____

_____

_____

_____

_____

_____

_____

_____

_____

What are the things you are most glad you tried? _____

Describe your mother in her best dress. _____

_____

_____

_____

_____

_____

_____

What similarities with your mother do you now see in

yourself or in your children? _____

_____

_____

_____

_____

_____

_____

_____

April

Describe your father in his working clothes. _____

_____

_____

_____

_____

_____

_____

What similarities with your father do you now see in
yourself or in your children? _____

_____

_____

_____

_____

_____

_____

_____

71

April

What did you like to do best with your childhood friends?

_____

_____

_____

_____

_____

_____

_____

_____

_____

_____

_____

_____

_____

_____

_____

_____

Share the recipe for one of your grandchildren's
favorite goodies they enjoy eating at your house.

_____

_____

_____

_____

_____

_____

_____

_____

_____

_____

_____

_____

_____

_____

MAY

To keep the heart unwrinkled,

to be hopeful,

kindly, cheerful, reverent –

that is to triumph

over old age.

THOMAS BAILEY ALDRICH

May

What are some special gifts you
have received over the years?

_____

_____

_____

_____

_____

_____

_____

_____

_____

_____

_____

_____

_____

_____

_____

_____

_____

What family traditions
do you want to pass on
to your grandchildren? _____

What is one of the most difficult choices you ever had

to make? _____

_____

_____

_____

_____

_____

_____

Would you make that same choice again? _____

_____

_____

_____

_____

_____

_____

_____

Do you remember a time when you ———————
felt particularly unsure or confused? ———————
What did you do? ———————

———————————————

———————————————

———————————————

———————————————

———————————————

———————————————

———————————————

———————————————

———————————————

———————————————

———————————————

———————————————

———————————————

———————————————

May

Did you ever go to a dance? _____

    Tell me about it. _____

_____

_____

_____

_____

_____

_____

Describe the most significant event you have ever attended.

_____

_____

_____

_____

_____

_____

_____

What kind of car did your family drive? _____

_____

_____

_____

_____

_____

_____

_____

Were you proud of it or embarrassed by it? _____

_____

_____

_____

_____

_____

_____

_____

Did you attend family reunions? _____

Share a memory of one. _____

_____

_____

_____

_____

_____

_____

_____

_____

_____

_____

_____

_____

_____

_____

May

What is your favorite season of the year? _____

    Why? _____

_____

_____

_____

_____

_____

_____

_____

_____

_____

_____

_____

_____

_____

_____

_____

Recall the first day of school for your children.

_____

_____

_____

_____

_____

_____

_____

_____

_____

_____

_____

_____

_____

_____

_____

_____

Tell me about your best childhood friend. _____

_____

_____

_____

_____

_____

_____

_____

_____

What advice would you _____

give your grandchildren _____

about choosing friends? _____

_____

_____

_____

_____

_____

_____

May

If you went to college or to a career training school, where did you go and why? _____

_____

_____

_____

_____

_____

_____

_____

_____

_____

_____

_____

_____

_____

_____

Describe the best
job and the worst
job you had in
your younger days.

_____

_____

_____

_____

_____

_____

_____

_____

_____

_____

_____

_____

_____

_____

_____

May

What were your youthful goals and ambitions for life?
Which ones have you been able to fulfill? _____

_____

_____

_____

_____

_____

_____

_____

_____

_____

_____

_____

_____

_____

_____

Are there certain Scriptures or other writings that you repeatedly turn to for inspiration and guidance?

_____

_____

_____

_____

_____

_____

_____

_____

_____

_____

_____

_____

_____

_____

_____

JUNE

Few things are more delightful

than grandchildren

fighting over your lap.

DOUG LARSON

June

If you learned to play a musical instrument, tell me about your memories of lessons, practice, recitals, and your music teacher. If not, what instrument did you always want to play and why? _____

_____

_____

_____

_____

_____

_____

_____

_____

_____

_____

_____

_____

_____

_____

What fashions were popular when you were in high school?

Did you like them? _____

Why or why not? _____

_____

_____

_____

_____

_____

_____

_____

_____

_____

_____

_____

_____

_____

_____

_____

How old were you when you met Grandpa, and what

attracted you to him? _____

_____

_____

_____

_____

_____

_____

When did you first know you wanted to marry him?

How did he propose? _____

_____

_____

_____

_____

_____

_____

_____

June

What did you wear on your wedding day? _____

What did Grandpa wear? _____

_____

_____

_____

_____

_____

_____

_____

_____

_____

_____

_____

_____

_____

June

Share a tradition from your _____

courtship that still remains special. _____

_____

_____

_____

_____

_____

_____

_____

_____

_____

_____

_____

_____

_____

_____

_____

_____

Share some advice on choosing a mate and marriage
that you wish to share with your grandchildren.

_____

_____

_____

_____

_____

_____

_____

_____

_____

_____

_____

_____

_____

_____

_____

Tell me about your
wedding day, from
beginning to end. _____

_____
_____
_____
_____
_____
_____
_____
_____
_____
_____
_____
_____
_____

Did your wedding ceremony include _____

a special vow to each other? _____

What was the significance of it? _____

_____

_____

_____

_____

_____

_____

_____

_____

_____

_____

_____

_____

_____

June

Where did you go on your honeymoon? _____

Share one humorous incident. _____

_____

_____

_____

_____

_____

_____

_____

_____

_____

_____

_____

_____

_____

_____

_____

_____

What was your first house or apartment together like?

_____

_____

_____

_____

_____

_____

_____

_____

_____

_____

_____

_____

_____

_____

Recall the special moments of _____

your children's wedding day. _____

_____

_____

_____

_____

_____

_____

_____

_____

_____

_____

_____

_____

_____

_____

What humorous moments do you recall from your wedding day? _____

_____

_____

_____

_____

_____

_____

_____

_____

_____

_____

_____

_____

_____

_____

_____

_____

_____

June

What do you love best about Grandpa now? _____

_____

_____

_____

_____

_____

_____

_____

_____

_____

_____

_____

_____

_____

_____

_____

_____

_____

Tell me about an anniversary celebration that was very special. _____

_____

_____

_____

_____

_____

_____

_____

_____

_____

_____

_____

_____

_____

_____

_____

JULY

And in the end,

it's not the years in your life

that count.

It's the life in your years.

ABRAHAM LINCOLN

Share a family tradition or memory _____
from the Fourth of July. _____

_____

_____

_____

_____

_____

_____

_____

_____

_____

_____

_____

_____

_____

_____

_____

Have you ever participated in a rally or demonstration?

What was the cause? _____

Share your feelings about it. _____

_____

_____

_____

_____

_____

_____

_____

_____

_____

_____

_____

_____

_____

_____

_____

_____

July

Who in your family served in the military and when?

Do you have a special memory of that person? ——

Did you learn to swim? _____

    At what age? _____

    How? _____

_____

_____

_____

_____

_____

_____

_____

_____

_____

_____

_____

_____

_____

_____

Did you take family vacations when growing up?

Record one memorable experience. _____

_____

_____

_____

_____

_____

_____

_____

_____

_____

_____

_____

_____

_____

_____

Tell about your first trip by plane, train, or ship.

How old were you? _____

Share your feeling about the experience. _____

_____

_____

_____

_____

_____

_____

_____

_____

_____

_____

_____

_____

_____

_____

July

If you ever traveled abroad, what was the most unique
experience of the trip? If not, what country would you
most like to visit? Why? _____

_____

_____

_____

_____

_____

_____

_____

_____

_____

_____

_____

_____

_____

What special trip have you taken with your grandchildren?

_____

_____

_____

_____

_____

_____

_____

_____

_____

_____

_____

_____

_____

_____

_____

Describe the most fascinating place you have visited.

_____

_____

_____

_____

_____

_____

_____

_____

_____

_____

_____

_____

_____

_____

_____

Tell about a driving trip with your children. _____

_____

_____

_____

_____

_____

_____

_____

_____

_____

_____

_____

_____

_____

_____

_____

_____

Did your relatives come to visit in the summer, or did you go to visit them? _____

_____

What are your memories of those visits? _____

_____

_____

_____

_____

_____

_____

_____

_____

_____

_____

_____

_____

How did you learn to drive? _____

_____

_____

_____

_____

_____

_____

Describe your first car. _____

_____

_____

_____

_____

_____

_____

_____

_____

July

Did a tragedy every strike your family? _____

How were you affected? _____

_____

_____

_____

_____

_____

_____

_____

_____

_____

_____

_____

_____

_____

_____

_____

_____

Share a favorite poem or a passage of writing that has been especially meaningful in your life. _____

_____

_____

_____

_____

_____

_____

_____

_____

_____

_____

_____

_____

_____

AUGUST

No cowboy was ever

faster on the draw than a

grandparent pulling a

baby picture out of a wallet.

AUTHOR UNKNOWN

What one special quality do you see in each of your
children and grandchildren? _____

_____

_____

_____

_____

_____

_____

_____

_____

_____

_____

_____

_____

_____

Did you have a collection when you were growing up?

_____

_____

_____

_____

_____

_____

_____

_____

What initially sparked your interest in it? _____

_____

_____

_____

_____

_____

_____

_____

_____

August

Describe a perfect summer day. _____

_____

_____

_____

_____

_____

_____

_____

_____

_____

_____

_____

_____

_____

_____

_____

_____

What kind of outdoor work do you like? _____

   Why? _____

_____

_____

_____

_____

_____

What kind of outdoor work do you dislike? _____

   Why? _____

_____

_____

_____

_____

_____

_____

What skills do you
want to pass down to
your grandchildren?

_____

_____

_____

_____

_____

_____

_____

_____

_____

_____

_____

_____

_____

_____

_____

_____

_____

August

When did you learn how to ride a bike, or to water ski, snow ski, roller skate, or sail? Share your memories of the experience. _____

_____

_____

_____

_____

_____

_____

_____

_____

_____

_____

_____

_____

_____

_____

August

What summer games and activities did your family enjoy?

_____

_____

_____

_____

_____

_____

_____

_____

_____

_____

_____

_____

_____

_____

_____

_____

Did you ever milk a cow or spend ———

time on a farm or in the country? ———

   Tell me about it. ———

_____

_____

_____

_____

_____

_____

_____

_____

_____

_____

_____

_____

_____

_____

_____

Describe your first trip alone. _____

_____

_____

_____

_____

_____

_____

_____

_____

_____

_____

_____

_____

_____

_____

_____

_____

What places would you still like to visit? _____

    Why? _____

_____

_____

_____

_____

_____

_____

_____

_____

_____

_____

_____

_____

_____

_____

_____

_____

August

Describe a frightening or difficult experience from childhood. _____

_____

_____

_____

_____

_____

_____

_____

_____

_____

_____

_____

_____

_____

_____

_____

_____

_____

Describe a frightening experience related to your children.

_____

_____

_____

_____

_____

_____

_____

_____

_____

_____

_____

_____

_____

_____

_____

_____   _____

Tell me about your most unforgettable summer experience as a child. _____

_____

_____

_____

_____

_____

_____

_____

_____

_____

_____

_____

_____

_____

List some of your favorite places to go on vacation.

_____

_____

_____

_____

_____

_____

_____

_____

_____

_____

_____

_____

_____

_____

SEPTEMBER

*Example is a lesson
that all can read.*

GILBERT WEST

september

Did you learn to sew or make other crafts? _____

How and when? _____

_____

_____

_____

_____

_____

_____

_____

What was the first thing you made? _____

_____

_____

_____

_____

_____

_____

Tell about a special outing you took with your mother or your father. _____

_____

_____

_____

_____

_____

_____

_____

_____

_____

_____

_____

_____

_____

What was the most tender day in your childhood? _____

_____

_____

_____

_____

_____

_____

_____

What was the most tender day as a mother? _____

_____

_____

_____

_____

_____

_____

_____

Share some
family rituals
when getting
ready to go
back to school.

september

As a young person did you volunteer for work in church
or the community? Tell me about it. _____

_____

_____

_____

_____

_____

_____

_____

_____

_____

_____

_____

_____

_____

_____

When did you move away from home? _____

_____

Describe where you lived _____

and how you felt about it. _____

_____

_____

_____

_____

_____

_____

_____

_____

_____

_____

_____

_____

Who was your best friend after you were married?

Describe some of the fun things you did together.

_____

_____

_____

_____

_____

_____

_____

_____

_____

_____

_____

Are you still friends? _____

_____

_____

Describe the time when you or your oldest sibling moved

away from home. _____

_____

_____

_____

_____

_____

_____

_____

How did it affect the rest of the family? _____

_____

_____

_____

_____

_____

_____

_____

September

What special talents did your parents nurture in you?

_____

_____

_____

_____

_____

_____

_____

How have you developed those talents? _____

_____

_____

_____

_____

_____

_____

What special talents
did you nurture in
your own children?

What is something _____

you learned from _____

an especially happy _____

time in your life? _____

_____

_____

_____

_____

_____

_____

_____

_____

_____

_____

_____

_____

What would you like to learn to do? _____

_____
_____
_____
_____
_____
_____
_____
_____

Why? _____

_____
_____
_____
_____
_____
_____
_____
_____
_____
_____

September

What would you do differently in life if you could? _____

_____

_____

_____

_____

_____

_____

_____

What would you do differently in parenting if you could?

_____

_____

_____

_____

_____

_____

_____

Describe your personal style in clothing, make up, skin care, and hair care. _____

_____

_____

_____

_____

_____

_____

_____

_____

_____

_____

_____

_____

_____

_____

_____

OCTOBER

A grandmother pretends

she doesn't know who you are

on Halloween.

ERMA BOMBECK

October

What do you like best about being a grandparent?
Why? _____

_____

_____

_____

_____

_____

_____

_____

_____

_____

_____

_____

_____

_____

_____

_____

_____

_____

How would you like to be remembered? _____

Why is this important to you? _____

_____

_____

_____

_____

_____

_____

_____

_____

_____

_____

_____

_____

_____

_____

What are some of the things that your grandchildren do that make you smile? _____

_____

_____

_____

_____

_____

_____

_____

_____

_____

_____

_____

_____

_____

_____

_____

What do you consider to be some _____
of life's most difficult challenges? _____

_____
_____
_____
_____
_____
_____
_____
_____

What is the most difficult challenge in raising kids?

_____
_____
_____
_____
_____
_____
_____

October

What do you consider to be life's greatest gifts? _____

_____

_____

_____

_____

_____

_____

_____

_____

_____

_____

_____

_____

_____

_____

_____

_____

What responsibilities did you parents require of you as
a child? Explain how this affected your growth and
development. _____

_____

_____

_____

_____

_____

_____

_____

_____

_____

_____

_____

_____

_____

When and where did you buy your first house?

Describe the house and explain _____
any significance it held for you. _____

_____

_____

_____

_____

_____

_____

_____

_____

_____

_____

_____

_____

_____

_____

_____

October

What is the strangest thing you have ever seen? _____

_____

_____

_____

_____

_____

_____

_____

_____

_____

_____

_____

_____

_____

_____

_____

_____

_____

_____

_____

Name your favorite hobby. _____

　　When and where did you start doing it? _____

_____

_____

_____

_____

_____

_____

Why do you enjoy doing it? _____

_____

_____

_____

_____

_____

_____

_____

Tell about a memorable hotel or resort you have visited.

Describe the location and the significance of the visit.

_____

_____

_____

_____

_____

_____

_____

_____

_____

_____

_____

_____

_____

_____

_____

Did you ever go on a hayride or bob for apples? _____

_____

_____

_____

What other fun fall activities _____

did you and your friends enjoy? _____

_____

_____

_____

_____

_____

_____

_____

_____

_____

_____

October

Tell about a significant illness you or someone in your family faced? How would the medical treatment differ now days? _____

_____

_____

_____

_____

_____

_____

_____

_____

_____

_____

_____

_____

_____

_____

Share some helpful home remedies or tips for good health. _____

_____
_____
_____
_____
_____
_____
_____
_____
_____
_____
_____
_____
_____
_____
_____

NOVEMBER

A candle loses

nothing by lighting

another candle.

AUTHOR UNKNOWN

What individuals have had the _____

greatest impact on your life? _____

    In what way? _____

_____

_____

_____

_____

_____

_____

_____

_____

_____

_____

_____

_____

_____

_____

What is your most treasured possession and why? _____

_____

_____

_____

_____

_____

_____

_____

_____

_____

_____

_____

_____

_____

_____

_____

_____

_____

_____

November

Who were your female role models when you were growing up? How have they affected the kind of person you are? _____

_____

_____

_____

_____

_____

_____

_____

_____

_____

_____

_____

_____

_____

What is your most vivid memory of being pregnant?

_____

_____

_____

_____

_____

_____

_____

_____

_____

_____

_____

_____

_____

_____

How did you choose your children's names? _____

_____

_____

_____

_____

_____

_____

_____

_____

Did you help name any of the grandchildren? _____

_____

_____

_____

_____

_____

_____

What family name
has been passed down
to other generations?
Any nicknames that
have been passed down?

_____

_____

_____

_____

_____

_____

_____

_____

_____

_____

_____

_____

November

What was a favorite _____

Thanksgiving tradition _____

in your family? _____

_____

_____

_____

_____

_____

_____

_____

_____

_____

_____

_____

_____

_____

_____

_____

What are some things from your childhood that
you are thankful for? _____

_____
_____
_____
_____
_____
_____
_____
_____
_____
_____
_____
_____
_____
_____
_____
_____

What childhood memory first comes to your mind
when you think about winter? _____

_____

_____

_____

_____

_____

_____

_____

_____

_____

_____

_____

_____

_____

_____

What is your most
poignant memory
about the childhood of
your own children?

November

What are some of the things you remember most about
your childhood friends? How many of those friends
still remain close today? _____

_____

_____

_____

_____

_____

_____

_____

_____

_____

_____

_____

_____

_____

What family recipe would you like to pass on to your children and grandchildren? _____

_____

_____

_____

_____

_____

_____

_____

_____

_____

_____

_____

_____

_____

_____

_____

What new tradition would you like to start in the family

with the grandchildren? What is it's significance? ———

_____

_____

_____

_____

_____

_____

_____

_____

_____

_____

_____

_____

_____

_____

Share a favorite Thanksgiving or Christmas recipe that
Grandpa would always request. _____

_____

_____

_____

_____

_____

_____

_____

_____

_____

_____

_____

_____

_____

_____

_____

_____

DECEMBER

Grandmas are moms

with lots of frosting.

AUTHOR UNKNOWN

Tell about some Christmas rituals in your family and how you felt about them. _____

_____

_____

_____

_____

_____

_____

_____

_____

_____

_____

_____

_____

_____

_____

Were you ever in a Christmas _____

program or Christmas parade? _____

Tell about that experience. _____

_____

_____

_____

_____

_____

_____

_____

_____

_____

_____

_____

_____

_____

_____

_____

December

What favorite Christmas treasures _____
have you kept from year to year? _____
    Share their origins. _____
_____
_____
_____
_____
_____
_____
_____

What Christmas ornaments do you remember making?
_____
_____
_____
_____
_____
_____
_____

Tell about a memorable Christmas visit with relatives.

_____

_____

_____

_____

_____

_____

_____

_____

_____

_____

_____

_____

_____

_____

_____

December

What is your favorite Christmas carol?

Why? *"Little Drummer Boy"*

**Did you have a Christmas stocking as a child
or a special ornament? What did it look like?**

We never had a Christmas
stocking. There were candy
and fruit put in paper
lunch bags (brown). These
early years where some
of the best in my life.

What is the first Christmas gift you remember receiving?

The first Christmas gift
I remember is a vest
sewed by Kathy (sister)
and mailed from Michigan.
Looking back in time,
the Beauty of Christmas
was being together as
a family. Mom cooked
a big dinner + baked
start bread.

Describe the Christmas that has
been the most meaningful to you
as a mom and as a grandmother.

The most meaningful
Christmas(s) to me
were and are the ones
with my children and
grandchildren. I can't
imagine life without
being able to watch
those little excited
faces on Christmas
morning & going
to Church the
evening before
(Christmas Eve). As
adults now it is
watching the grandchilds
I am thankful that
the children live close
by.

What would be the most wonderful gift you could receive? The most wonderful gift I could receive would be... my children & their families putting God at the center of everything in their life. That they would/will hear & read God's word & live by God's guidance in all things. For my offspring to marry men & women who are Godly equally yoked.

Why? → Why? If they live their lifes with their goal living in heaven when they leave this world.

195

December

What is something that you and
Grandpa enjoy doing together?

_____

_____

_____

_____

_____

_____

_____

_____

_____

_____

_____

_____

_____

_____

_____

What would you like to see

happen in the next ten years? _____

_____

_____

_____

_____

_____

_____

_____

_____

_____

_____

_____

_____

_____

_____

_____

Did you ever surprise someone else? _____

In what way? _____

_____

_____

_____

_____

_____

_____

_____

Did you ever get surprised by someone, maybe for your

birthday or anniversary? _____

_____

_____

_____

_____

_____

_____

What was one of the best surprises you ever had?

A gift? This book (Barbary Hay Looney)

An unexpected favor? Ray Looney
(Thelma's husband)

I was a senior
and had no money to
buy a HS class ring.
Ray told me if I would
hoe the potatoes at the upper
end of the flat (Ronnie's
house now sets there) he
would buy my class-ring
for me. It was getting
dusk & heard someone
hoeing next to me (it
was Ray) he told me
he would furnish to
go on to the house;
but not to tell Thelma.

December

What word best describes your life? An ocean wave

Explain why. Ocean waves come in different sizes, small, medium & large. Some can be ½ foot to 35 feet high.

When things were good with my husband/household the small waves would represent that. Problems, troubles, sick children, lack of money, lack of enough food, lack of enough clothes, these were the medium to high waves. Things were rough.

(8-25-08) My Godly given patience, faith and perseverence, His guidance & love, has gotten me through life. God also placed certain people in my life to love & support me.

200

What advice about life do you want all of your family to remember? "Love a lot", forgiveness & compassion (108) for everyone.

Special Memories

Use the following pages to share special family stories,
words of wisdom, more stories about yourself,
or words of love you would like to be passed down
to your children and grandchildren.

_____

_____

_____

_____

_____

_____

_____

_____

_____

_____

_____

_____

_____

_____

Special Memories

Special Memories

Special Memories

Photos

Photos

Photos

MomMom

Gran

babica or stara mama (Slovenian)

Grand-me're (French)

bubbe (Yiddish)

obaasan (Japanese)

Granny

Grandma

Nonnie

Mimi

abuelita (Spanish)

MeeMaw

Grandmama

Marmie

MawMaw

nonna (Italian) Mamme (Greek)

babushka (Russian) Sitto (Arabic)

Nana

baka (Croatian)

Nanny

oma (German)

MomMom

babica or stara mama (Slovenian)

Grand-me're (French)

obaasan (Japanese)

Gran Gran

bubbe (Yiddish)

Granny

Grandma

Mimi

abuelita (Spanish)

Marmie

MawMaw

MeeMaw

Grandmama

babushka (Russian) Sitto (Arabic)

nonna (Italian) Mamme (Greek)

Nana

baka (Croatian)

Nanny

oma (German)